BEING HERE

BOOKS BY RICHARD WEHRMAN

Talking To The Wind

The Book of the Garden

Light was Everywhere: Poems by Richard Wehrman

Dialogues with Death

BEING HERE

POETIC INQUIRIES

RICHARD WEHRMAN

Merlinwood Books • East Bloomfield, NY

Richard Wehrman's books may be purchased through
his website at www.richardwehrman.com, or through
the online booksellers—www.amazon.com or
www.barnesandnoble.com.

Published by
Merlinwood Books
P.O. Box 146
E. Bloomfield NY 14443

www.richardwehrman.com

To all those confused, dumbfounded, and amazed
by Existence.

TABLE OF CONTENTS

FOREWORD

Many of us now are struggling with what seems to be the increasingly tightening and binding consensus world view. There is a growing sense in many people that this prevailing view is not the only truth or even a truth. The writer of this book—or is he the scribe, writing down what is emerging—is inquiring into a way to live into the world. The method is simple, though not easy. It involves quieting, listening, allowing, letting it come forth while paying attention. The rhythm is slow and deliberate. It is the rhythm of the backyard, of the breeze, of turning leaves. It travels along boundaries: between sleeping and waking, between seeing and being seen, writing and being written, losing and finding. It wanders. It looks and feels for a true face of things. It insists on looking into that face itself; the accounts of others will not do, not really, not in the heart. It requires a stripping down, feeling along in the dark, no known path. There is suffering and doubt, and joy.

Though it is a unique work, I find its desire and demand has some correspondence with this:

> God, the world, everything can pass into nothingness,
> victims of nihilistic constructions, metaphysical doubts,
> despairs of every sort. What remains when all perishes
> is the face of things as they are. When there is nowhere
> to turn, turn back to the face before you, face the world.
> (James Hillman, *Thought of the Heart*)

Being with these meditations requires slowing down, being patient, reflecting. The rewards are in the discovery of its many hidden gems.

In gratitude to Richard for this work,

—PAUL KUHL, *Rochester, NY*

BEING HERE

BEGINNING

He realized that something
was needed, an introduction,
a way to make what
followed comprehensible,
and of course he wondered,
was that even possible? Yet
he knew he had to try, to
set guideposts, to point out
that these *were not* poems,
not in the way that others, or
himself, thought of poems—
he needed to be clear,
these words were a meditation,
an exploration, an out-flowing
let loose as the pencil was
set to paper, where the
present-moment-awareness
allowed to arise whatever
came forth, as long as
he allowed it, did not subvert
it, did not structure its arising,
that it expressed *its own*
being—which was his being
as well—that it be done
in the presence of all that held
him, and all that he beheld,
without exception, without
expectation, and he hoped,
would be blessed by the
clarity of the light of what is.

BEING HERE

He woke, and in
waking was refreshed,
by the breeze, though
the day was warm,
hot in the sun that
fell upon his feet, on
the glass table top
that bore his books;
and the tinnitus, ringing
from the haze of the hill,
gathered around him,
while the gray-green
of the massed trees,
monumental, sang with
a high-pitched whine,
an after-tone like
bells built by bees, and
he breathed it in,
the glorious unmoving
wonder of life, of being,
of being *here*, intimately
himself, the taste of
all that is, drinking it in,
swallowing it down,
life itself, though the only
movement was the
leaves, was the light
streaming the heat, the
being, into his heart and
out, breath after breath.

THE BLOSSOM

He sat and remembered
his friend, whom he met years
ago, who was now—he had
been told—in her bed dying.
He felt how she had entered
his heart, had remained
there, though their contact
was infrequent; the way her
memory blossomed when
heart-mind brought her forth,
and he wondered how this
could be, how the heart could
hold those whom he loved in
aliveness, even *the dead*, who,
when recalled by desire or
by love, were alive in the heart.
His gaze shifted to the field,
to the horses who grazed
in the damp rain, feeling the
radiance, the warmth emerge
and encircle him, as he
held it all—his own being,
the world that held him,
his heart that held hers in her
dying, as the breeze moved
the leaves, as the day held the
moment that in its time
would blossom, would again
become night, and once more,
a new day.

THE WARMTH

What, he asked, was this
long journey into the Self?
He felt the warmth and
the richness of poets who
seemed to belong to the past,
yet as he held their books and
read their names: Bly, Neruda,
Jimenez, Kabir, Rilke, Rumi—
he felt the warmth rise again
in his chest, a deepening of
love, a presentiment of his
own death, his body's passing
away; all this, as he gazed on
the blue sky and the white
clouds, as the silence brought
him what it brought everyone—
solace, the sound of a single
bird, the crisp beginning of
morning's freshness—and with
these gifts he could do nothing
but bow down, offer gratitude
to behold it all, to be part
of the giving that arose
unasked, and kept continually
arising.

THE LIGHT

She lay there, in the bed where
she had been lain, with the window
before her, and the light streaming—
or it may have been a wall, but still,
somehow, without any way, any
possibility, the light streamed, and
she smiled, unknowing in the
warmth, in the gold of the glow that
drew her, out of herself, as she
became, though others did not see it,
and others swore they did, the light
as it returned, streaming and weaving,
into the flow of the gold that came
down, as it came in, as it arose and
went out, hand-over-hand, held
and beheld, each particle of gold,
as the light came down, as her light
rose up, as she—*who she was*, not
the one she had never been, but the
true golden one, the beloved one,
the loving one, grew smaller as a body,
then smaller still, as *she*, the indivisible,
the unnamable, the unseeable, grew
larger, grew greater, became the
vastness, the all-that-is, and left
behind, residue or gift, for those
who could see with an inner eye,
who could feel, who would come
to awaken in the night to that which
they could never encompass, believe,
or acknowledge as their anguish
fell away: an embrace, a lovingness
within, a gift from the infinite
to the finite: her blessing.

WAKING UP

He woke again, as he always
did, out of nothing and into
something; the wind woke too,
barely there, a dry exhale of
breath over the leaves,
over the dry grass, and he noted
how complete he felt, in this
almost not hereness, only the
edge of awareness, the quality
that noted, that attended to,
and beyond that nothing else
at all, though it was coming back,
the body's sense of being, his
buttocks sore in the chair where
he had slept, and the single
sounds that arrived before
sight, for he had not yet opened
his eye—so a single scrape,
a rough-edged rasp, which carried
no meaning, any more than
(was it the sound of a bird?)...
he could not tell; just the arrival
of sound, before you called it
sound, and it was just it,
what-it-was, and now he opened
his eyes, and the hill streamed in,
simply in that moment was,
where before it was not, as it
was again as his eyelids closed,
and the heat of the sun on his legs
as the bird, a different one,
called three single cries,
and as the wind moved again,
and he smiled.

WHAT THEN

He realized, as he massaged
his swollen ankles, that he
talked to himself and to
others as though he would
be here forever; that his words
carried no weight, and could
be endlessly revised, with
truer thoughts, more real
thoughts; in this way he could
be frivolous with his time,
his speech, his activities, his
diversions and entertainments,
and he did not consider until
now, as he stroked his ankles,
misshapen and painful,
that endings had an actual end,
that what seemed eternal
was in fact finite, that his
mouth would stop moving mid-
sentence, that the sun would
set one last time, that time
itself would run down, the
candle burn all there was to
burn, and this sobered him, for
his gallows humor had always
included tomorrow, and if
now it did not, what then?

TRAVELING

He was surprised
to see the gray clouds,
for the sunrise was clear
with blue sky, and he
assumed, as he always had,
that the sky moved
as the sun moved, east
to west, yet here the clouds
came, traveling west to
east, and he thought of
the trajectory he imagined
his life took, of birth
to death, infancy to old age,
and he wondered if he
had missed something,
if the winds moved
differently than he supposed,
if death also traveled
toward life, if there were
more currents than he
could imagine, and if
imagining itself, setting
a distinct course, one he
planned in advance, kept
him from seeing; if he
were at this moment
actually growing younger,
at the same time he grew
older; if he was in fact
moving in ways he could
barely sense, into another
life, into other worlds.

CLEARED AWAY

Again it occurred,
the waking up from
a dozing off, and the
space returned to had
been emptied, cleaned of
the debris of the mind—
the worries, the thoughts;
and what remained
was incredible freshness,
the new that did not
announce or proclaim,
only the sense of endless
supporting space, allowing
anything, ready to supply
whatever was needed to
accomplish; there would
be room, and then room
itself would be cleared
away, wiped clean and
made ready for whatever
else wanted to come.

WHAT HE HAD

Could he really lay
it down, he wondered,
all the accumulated
projected desires, partly
his own, but most of it laid
out by others, in books,
in talks, in teachings
that said, *this* is your goal:
the unattainable, the
spiritually pure—you, the
ignorant, the unwashed and
uneducated—this is your
way to become better
than you inherently are.
No sense that you were
what you were meant to be,
only what you might
be molded to, chiseled into,
added on to your skeletal
frame of lack and loss.
For laid down, what would
he have but himself,
the very thing they convinced
him was worthless the
way it was.
What if this was all
he had, all he was?
What then?

LEAVING

Could he, he asked again,
walk out into the desert
of himself, let his self go,
the one built by the labor
of lifetimes—this one—
drop away into the ageless
void; and as he asked, he
knew: this is what it comes
to anyway, tonight as he
slept, or tomorrow, as the
result of old age, a natural
death, that waited closer
each day, a wordless chant,
it will all go, all of it,
castles and skyscrapers of
who you are, who you built
yourself to be; it ends at
the end—that's the idea—you
step from *here*, your
construction, into *there*,
the body abandoned—and
you saw it was not a despair,
but a ship to be boarded,
that old kind of being
unmoored, as your ship of
free being sails.

THE FLOW

He awoke to the knowing
that though he wished for it all,
his creativity, his knowing and
beingness, to all flow out—as
these words did from the pencil's
lead—from the formlessness
to form, with no struggle, with
no effort, like water running
down the side of a mountain,
that there were pools,
blockages and backwaters,
that the flow would apparently
stop, but in fact it wouldn't, it
couldn't; the flow was a filling up
as well as a flowing down, and
once the rim was reached, any
obstruction breached, the flow
flowed on, that it did so effortlessly,
by simply doing what it did: fill
and flow, and those blockages
gave the flow its power,
its force. By which—being itself—
overcame what others, what
he himself had seen as obstacles,
as points of confusion, as the
end of the flow, and it was
none of these, for the flow filled
and filled, perhaps for days, or
months, or years—who knew,
maybe even lifetimes, but always,
always, it could be no other
way, it flowed over, it flowed on,
it flowed unending, past the

edges of time itself—and knew
itself at last in its effulgence
as being, as life itself, as
creativity, as who one was and
beyond names would always be.

UNRECOGNIZABLE

He searched for certainty
in an uncertain world;
he looked at the unseen,
and since it was unseen,
sought to bring it near,
to refine its sharpness,
to make it holdable, to
find tangibility. His
efforts all failed; he sought
to make water solid, to
give soul a distinct form,
to quantify love so that
he could hold it in a box,
to carry it with him.
His efforts all failed.
With every new attempt
he saw the outcome, his
patterns became transparent,
yet he still walked familiar
paths; only old age
seemed to offer help, taking
away his capacities; the
way simple things were
strangely unfamiliar, the
way one thing became
another, without his knowing
how. Only unknowableness
seemed to offer any
way in, to bring him,
unexpectedly, relief from
his mind.

ALL THE WAY IN

Sitting in the shifting
sun and shade of the
afternoon trees, all he
could feel was perfection,
and out of his contentment
wondered why this
was so, that when he
was content, it was total
contentment, and then later,
when it was discontent, or
agitation, or dissatisfaction—
then it was total dissatisfaction.
He saw how he yearned
for the uncomfortable
to go away, to be changed
in a moment's decision
to something he liked,
something more pleasant.
But it did not work
that way; when he was in,
he was *all the way in*,
when he was out, it was
all out. The breeze shifted
around his fingers, sounds of
the harvester drifted up from
the distant field, and as
the insects hummed he put
down his pencil, he
closed his eyes.

Still the perfection persisted,
as the silence he woke
out of was reflected all
about him, in the depth
of the space that extended
unendingly, wherein the
sounds of the leaves, the birds,
the cock crowing all were
distantly soft and clear,
as clear as minnows darting
in the rippled water of
a mountain creek, the
sights and sounds an inter-
penetration of his soul and
theirs, but there was no
his and *theirs*, they were
one emptiness, pristine and
clear as the sky, as the
orange light of the backlit
leaves of the vine as it climbed
the bare bark of the pine,
moving in the chime of
the church bell's resonate reach
over miles, flowing in the ear
of the earth as he sat, no
one in particular, receiver
of all particulars, as the gift
they were, flowing out
of the infinite flow, into this
moment, unending.

LETTING IT GO

The day that started
so well ended in frustration,
as he disappointed himself,
setting the bar too high,
then beginning the old
habit of judgment: what
he did wrong; so now as
he sits in the evening sun
it lets itself go, the
critical edge sinks away,
and he sees the judgments
as a holding on, how some-
thing *wants* to hold on,
the way they make him who
he is—or was. Giving up
is always losing, and he sees
how he wants to hold fast,
even to the ugly or painful,
where he can trace the
lines of his face, *his face*,
not an emptiness;
but the sinking away
won't allow it. It's time
for all that to go; to face
whatever he is without himself,
the old one who chooses to
make errors, who sins in
order *to be*. And so he lets go.
No, he doesn't:
He does.

AS IT IS

The clear morning offered
no way in; every attempt
to write was pulling something
whole apart, into pieces
that resisted their disintegration.
It was like taffy, elastic, or
like water that when scooped in
the hand ran back into the
stream. He could discriminate
the continuous drone of
the cicadas, but by themselves,
what were they? It was best
to leave all as it was, as
it is, for it cannot be separated
anyway. Even his words, as
he watched them emerge
on the page, had a mystery of
integration: at first they were
not there, then, all on their own
they appeared, a trail of
looped carbon between ruled lines.
He stopped and looked up,
settled, and sought to describe
it—the peace, the integration—but
could not. The world just was,
and whatever it was,
he was too.

THE THIRD

Part of him didn't like
the direction the writing
had taken; it seemed too
philosophical, it lacked
the conciseness of insight,
and he was confused by
the third person, the one
who seemed to observe,
who neglected the first
person, the one he spent
so much time with, that he
had been intimate with as
long as he could remember.
This *third* who wrote,
seemed a relation to his
critical voice, though he
noticed there was more
observation than criticism;
he felt part of this voice
came from *The Death
Of Virgil*, and that bothered
him, the way the words
seemed to slide from those
pages onto these, and he
wondered how that was;
were they not different people,
was he not his own individual
being? Yet the words kept
coming, and he found
himself more interested
in what they said than in
their manner of speaking. . .

MOISTURE

This morning the humidity
lies heavily on everything,
dampness seeps in, the entire body
feels saturation, and the mind
craves the opposite of what is:
dryness, clarity, a slight
chill to move the body into
action, to get the blood flowing.
These opposites hold great
desire; love for this lethargic
humidity is hard to bring forth,
except in times of exceeding
dryness! In ancient times
we came forth from such
moistness; once we swam in
our mother's womb—is
this what we seek to deny?
The body is filled with this
moisture: mucus, phlegm, and
blood—urine and tears. Are these
the moistures we avoid on dry
land? All life swims in this
ocean; we were not given life as
rocks, stones, or gems. Some
virtue of movement and
merging, of an ability to sink in,
is deep within who we are.
Not loving what we are—
that is the driest hell of all.

TIME OVERDUE

Always, first, was the image,
a vague sense with no vagueness
about it, of stone riding on
stone, a continual shift,
the shelves sliding, bone
upon bone, rock itself flowing
like water, like blood, like
oil, the beloved of hydraulics,
all of it moving, over the
resistance, the force of the
way we wanted it to be, but it
wouldn't, it couldn't, it had
to move, the centrifugal
wind, and we felt it, in the
pit of the stomach, the ache,
the pain, of the having to be, the
birth, overlooked, now upon us,
full term; we knew it was
time, the time overdue, the
balance due, and the payment
demanded, here at the crossroads,
already crossed, we could
no longer see—see them, for
the storm clouds were dark,
and the rain, for which we had
waited, the rain and the
cold and the dark were coming.

THE BITTERNESS OF DESIRE

There was no way, he saw,
that he could really do for
others, unless their desires
and his own overlapped, and
he had within his soul the
capacity to act, and that acting
be to fill his own desire. His
inherent selfishness no longer
allowed him to act, as he had
thought he did—selflessly,
and it filled him with
disappointment, to see that
while in this body, he was not
a saint, a bodhisattva—most
of the time not even a *kind* man,
but one who had given up
on changing himself for
the better. Oh, he was capable
of small gestures, particularly
where they would enhance
his vision of himself as
someone other than who he
really was, as an organic bodily
being. His soul perhaps understood
there was some chance of
advancement, where he could do
penance and repentance, could
grieve his own venal nature.
But this was a bitter, unwelcome
pill, and he had no water with
which he could swallow.

WHAT WANTS TO COME

Out of that space that she
could not command, could
not direct, could extract
nothing from, except what
was given by the space itself,
out it came—what wanted
to come in its own way—and
she the bystander, the observer,
the one along on the hurtling
ride, though the space itself
was Silence itself, unmoving,
unmoved, unmovable—yet
it drew her in, into its very
within, she who had been with-
out, powerless, hands pressed
against the glass of its sides,
like Alice to the looking-glass,
then she fell, was lifted in,
was absorbed into the all she
saw, the all that was that is,
heard, smelled, touched, tasted,
though none of these senses
were, only the clear light,
yellow on the impending fall,
flooding the field, the transition
of the seasonal air, as Summer
shimmered into non-existence,
and clarity stood in silent
reveling: color and light and
form, falling upon her all.

EACH ONE WAS

He could see it in the
clear cloudless air, in the
silence, how each one
was the doorway in,
opening onto unknown
worlds, known only in the
heart, by the heart's eye, in
our attraction to each other;
how there was no special
one: how each one *was*
the one, unique among all
others, all others complete
uniqueness as well, awaiting
the eye of the heart to
fall upon them, yet content
if it did not, and when
opened, each revealing the
one thing each heart knew
was needed: this unknown,
unrecognized, gloriously
alien universe of what one
thought *one was not*—now,
here *I am*, and the other in
me, revealing to the beloveds
what they could not conceive,
how heart-to-heart opens
the channel, the worm hole
between, the movement of
world into world expanding
and growing, love into love,
deep, beyond every star
in the infinite sky.

CLOUDLESS

His most frequent access
was the border where sleep
emerged into wakefulness,
where the boundary was thin,
and action was not directed
by his lesser being; here,
he stepped over, or the over
stepped here into the world.
The sense of the particular
ways delineated by the ordinary
mind seemed suspended,
inoperative, and only the
clear freedom of *no fixed*
way was present, so that
movement could slide where
it wished, and possibility
was present in every particle
of air: clean, refreshed,
new as the cloudless blue sky.
This was as far as he could go,
to be aware at this threshold, to
let its influence, its aliveness,
pour into him, to trust
that what could be carried
would be carried, forward into
the actions of the day, and to
allow whatever came forth
from this edge-less boundary,
to be exactly whatever it
wanted to be.

THE TOWN

He discovered there was a city
in his heart, perhaps more of
a town, certainly a community,
of which he was fully unaware
before; and within that town, in
harmony of togetherness and
aloneness, all those he loved
lived. He had not noticed them
move in; he had waved them
away as they climbed aboard their
trains to leave, thinking they
traveled to the mountains, or
the seaside, or to other countries
to retire. Over the years he
missed them, some more than
others, but all of them, when he
was true to himself, were beloved.
He never received a postcard;
perhaps he thought they had all
died. After all, he was an old man
himself, waiting his turn from
the night visitor. So his surprise
was astonishment, when he turned
and discovered each one within,
beautiful and living in his own
heart, where they waited to
welcome him home, and where
none would ever leave.

SYMPHONY

Oh bright sky, blue,
blossoming between
brilliant yellow-green,
waxed white pin-oaked
fingers, feathering in breeze-
blown Canandaiguan air,
whispering your mid-day
cricket singing symphony
full-stop, breathing
again the billion leaf-
shifting slide, shimmering
obeisance, of the lifting-
falling-sliding god-dance
of the particular day;
called by and within the knock-
empty slack sounds startled
earward in the clarity-filled
air, hummed by dry
dragged rhythm-rasping
wheat upon the tree-fringed
hills, where electric bore and
hammer bangs bring forth
old weather beaten barns
repair, white butterflys
remark upon the spiny
thorns of thistles, giving up
the all of Autumn's soon
arrival, as the cock calls out
above the twit and chitter,
birds all sing and say:
Today! Today!

COMFORTABLE

He kept finding himself
in a situation of feeling
totally comfortable, and
that made him uncomfortable.
Such ease and relaxation had
to be a false state, a conditional
condition: one of temperature,
sunlight, or lack of distress;
it couldn't be something he
should become used to, to
expect it to be there all the
time, for he had become used
to the dis-comfort of things,
the un-rightness, the difficulties
that extended around him;
that the basis of the universe
was pain and suffering, that
ease was an illusion. But now,
as he gazed through the warm
haze of the late September
day at the golden rise of the hill
before the trees, as the crows
cawed and the crickets sawed
their late afternoon song,
he saw, he felt, *he was* and was
filled with satisfaction and
ease; he knew *this* as reality, as
truth, in this moment; its
reality *was*, as much as any
other, and in this moment there
was no other, only the wind as
it warmed and caressed, as what is
came in, as it settled down,
as it announced itself with a
whisper as love.

GOURMET

Some can
take a life
and consume it
as a morsel;
flipping
through the pages,
wandering through
the stacks,
looking for
another life,
as delicious
as the last.

Seeing the photographs
disturbed him. Who was
this old man, overweight,
neck thick like a plucked
chicken thigh, staring out
at the lake behind dark
glasses, under a farmer's
faded long-billed cap?
Not the one he saw in the
mirror as he shaved, the
cross between Hemingway
and Harrison; twenty-
five years younger, forty
pounds lighter. Of course
the mirror reflected only his
self-imagined upper quarter;
his lower Saggitarian was
a stumbling draft horse,
serviceable but not svelte.
But these wrinkled baggy
clothes? These slouching
pouched eyes and the
thin white cropped hair?
His wife had chanced upon
some park-side bum, washed
up by life and ready to be
done. Pictures do not lie—
someone somewhere told him.
But this picture held it up
and asked him: Who's
the liar here—him, or you?

THE SLUMBERING TREES

As he relaxed he was amazed
again at how easy it was, the
relaxation did it all, and all it
did was release what was not
really there, but the mind in its
obsession created: the ghost
castle of delusions, illusions,
manufactured fear—and it
crumbled away, that which was
so solid in the hours before dawn,
and reality reasserted the way
things were, as the gray sky met
the fringed edge of the still
slumbering trees, as the yellow
leaves patterned the still-green
grass, as the comfort of
acceptance settled into his
body, saturating every cell,
sinking on through, lending his
weight to the earth, that received
him as itself, and he joined in the
gratitude of all being, no longer
being himself, as he had known
himself, the tension of boundaries
and resistances, but as air,
as capacity, as whatever the
moment brought him to be.

BONFIRE

Perhaps, he thought,
there should be a great
burning, a bonfire, a
harvest fire at the edge
of the field, the year
thrown in, old accumulations
all, and so much more
from the years before, the
efforts added on, flammables,
fire-filled flaming on
an October night, and
the more added the more
found to be carried in,
old aches and enmities,
attitudes, personal opinions,
the way you know, you
knew, everything was—
all of it dry and crisp,
ready for the red-reaching
flames, eating it all, flakes
of spark dancing in the
dark sky, and the roaring
voice out of the flaming
heat-white raising:
It is done, it is done,
it is done!

UNDEFINED

The day's timelessness puzzled
him; he could distinguish the
days of the week with a
calendar, but Tuesday felt
like Friday, felt like Saturday;
morning and afternoon as well,
the sunlight shifted to different
positions, the temperature had
a different feel, but it all felt
curiously undifferentiated,
as though he were receding
further into space and the
silence, yet everything was
distinct and present, simply as
though an old kind of meaning,
the old definitions of things
were draining away, leaving
only what was there in a new
way, one with less emotions, or
associations, and this even as
his memory of previous events
sharpened, in some way was
more distinct; he gazed at the
goldenrod, the white petals of the
wildflowers in the near field, and
felt not beauty—but a warm
reassurance, as though held by
the incomprehensible profligate
nature of creation; that even
as it left, proclaimed its
unchallengeable power to stay.

TRANSFORMATION

He used to worry about
becoming distracted, of not
being able to be single-minded,
of holding his thoughts and
intentions in a single direction,
where they gathered force
and became unified; now as
he watched, his thoughts did
none of that, they slid slowly
one into another, shifting
and changing shape the way
clouds do in the sky. He
could start in one place, and
end up in entirely another;
what was large became small,
what was small sometimes
disappeared completely.
He saw these were not random
thoughts he was following,
they often would lead to
revelation—or, mysteriously,
into clarity and spaciousness
where no thoughts existed at all,
just as he continually was
fascinated by the way words
emerged from the tip of his
pencil as he wrote,
without foreknowledge,
and then when he stopped,
they disappeared, just
like now.

NOTHING STEPPED BACK

The Silence was so complete,
so all-encompassing, so filled
with the absolute infusion
of love, that she could only
marvel at the astonishment
that was completely inactive,
dense with contentment and
peace, as each thing beheld
held all the rest, as nothing
stepped back from love,
but was composed of it, brought
it forth as every atom joined,
no love lost, all gathered in,
never gone but waiting, in
this space that knew no time,
for where was there to go when
everywhere and every time
was *here*; and it all changed
as she watched, and was
all the same, and she felt the
warm astonishment of every
love loved here in this moment,
and the grief was—if love
could be grief in any way—that
she did not see it, did not know it,
that what before were words
was the reality, that no love left,
all were here, all loss was
gained, love *was* the particles
of existence, her actual being,
her reciprocal gift from God.

THE BIRTH

So he understood that *he*
was *she*, that the beloved
sought for so long was *she*
himself, and in their joining,
in their consummation of
intimacy, that was that
word's source, came forth as
the Child, the Christ, the shining
Self for whom they had longed
for so long, and they—he and
she—dissolved in the child's
being, each stepped forth
as themselves, each joined
in the bliss of the other, that
was no longer other, but to
each their own beloved being,
radiant with such intensity
that each being incorporate
upon the earth became themselves,
and that light, that *being*,
was recognized, was seen, was
known by *the light in their eyes*,
joined with his own, her own,
and the world was seen as
the love it was, offering itself to
them, coming into being
through them: love
loving love became love.

THE LEAVES

The leaves always talked
to him, suggesting he settle
down, let go of his anxious
whirling and concerns about
what was being done when;
he had difficulty beginning
if he had no idea where
he was going, or of what
would come next; the fear
arose of not being prepared,
of being caught in the open,
vulnerable to attack. It was
as though he lived in a time
of war, and he wondered if
these feelings arose from
another life—as though this
one was not enough, that the
attacks of criticisms and
corrections were not as damaging
as bombs. So the leaves knew
and he trusted their good
intentions, the way they looked
down at him, and up at the sky
at the same time; they heard the
bells from the old church,
just as he did, and were formed
of a similar wisdom and
love—of letting go, of relaxing,
of dropping the war that
raged only in his mind.

HE LISTENED

He saw there was nothing to
do with the blue sky, no act to
perform with the leaves speaking
in the high branches, nowhere
to take the fallen leaves curled
into brown upon the dry grass;
they as well needed nothing from
him, other than his presence,
his being, which was not his
to take away, to withhold, to
give to some other. They were
each the all of it, arising wherever
arising occurred; they filled the
silence with their *being* silence,
his silence and theirs were the
same. The dancing sunlight,
the sounds of men making and
doing in the world—these also
were the silence sounding itself,
calling to him in his semi-separation,
whispering the right way, the way
to slide in to that which was out,
to enfold them all and to be
enfolded, to hold hands all the
way back to the beginning, and
ahead to the infinite yet-to-be,
intimately each the all. And
the sky remained blue, and the
birds called, as he, and all the
leaves above him, listened.

HORSES

Horses galloping on the
hill—bright sun, blue
sky, joy on an autumn
morning. Gensei says,
"With the happiness held
in one inch-square heart,
you can fill the whole space
between heaven and earth."
Looking around me, feeling
within, my desires are only
what appears before me,
my gratitude as boundless
as the cool air. When I
was younger, *this* is what
I searched for, believing
it to be a treasure-world
of fantastical appearance;
now as the satisfaction
of being fills every pore,
my only regrets are the
pains I've caused others.
When the smallest of the
small is more than enough,
I am filled with both joy
and sorrow, tears, and a
smile wider than the
widest sky.

THE GOAL OF FOG

After reading a few poems
by Ryokan, he found himself
sinking into the silent world;
everyday worries faded away
before they ever began. The
morning haze, after the evening
rain, gives a green softness to
all he sees, all he hears.
Contentment puzzles him, and
he feels, "Why do anything?"
Still, he is at peace with that
feeling. Yet he knows the day
will unfold into activity, and
that will be fine as well. He
remembers the carrot and the
stick, how he always kept some
goal before him, just out of
reach. Now the goal fades, as
the morning's damp fog reveals
the world that is already present
and given, and he wanders
without anxiety from one thing
to the next. In his heart he feels
the community of all those he
loves. Yet right now, of the most
importance, is the blue jay
calling in the distance, and the
changing colors of the leaves,
and the tiny spheres of rain
water, lined one after the other,
upon each bending
blade of grass.

IT CAME

He sat in the early morning
hours before dawn, noticing
the way time's structure was
slipping away, losing its old
boundaries, the confines of
the demarcations of the clock,
though he could feel the
heaviness in his eyelids, the
easy way he could slide back
into sleep, as he stared at the
black windows waiting for
the light. Slow cars drifted
by in the darkness, the sounds
of their engines muffled by
the closed windows, the glass,
the drapes opened to nothing
he could see, but that he knew
was coming—the shift out of
the old repetitive dreams
into something newer, that
his mind said was just another
day, but that he, the real he,
knew was an unknown being,
already forming itself, out
there in the formless dark,
that withheld its revealing until
all was the only way it could
be for this particular day,
and like a cloud, forming out
of empty air—with the light,
it came.

BRILLIANCE

The sun, brilliant, struck
my eyes, so that there danced,
invisible to others, its burnt
effect, bright upon my retina;
I blinked, and all was black,
but for the dancing icon
blurred and bright, that slid
across the darkness of my
interior eye—then open on
the page before me superseded
all, and hid beneath its bright
out-casting words of meaning,
saying—"See! I am the One
above the all, the burning bush,
the flame before all standing
firm shall fall; one glance
upon my face and you are
wiped away; bow down, relent,
and see how slow I fade;
you fear to face me now that
you may never see again,
aught but my brightness
burned—look now, that fire
is placed upon and in, all that
you can see: I Am the fire alive
in every single thing: be burnt by
my bright light and come and
live with me."

CUTTING WOOD

The silence flooded in after
the chainsaw stopped, and he
pulled the plugs from his ears,
allowing the wind to resume its
speech, which had never ceased,
but flowed over him and the piston
bangs of the saw, caring nothing
for his noise; it was his affair if
he traded the bliss of the autumn
afternoon air, the clear colors of
the yellow gold, green, and orange-
sienna for the racket that turned
tree trunks into coarse sawdust
and eighteen-inch logs. Some
things needed doing, winter would
come, snow would bury the
long limbs felled by the storm,
the one that split the old locust and
dropped half the tree across the
ditch, the one that caught the
runoff from the rain—slowly filling
with tiny maples and birch, over
which deer stumbled to chew
the ragged stumps of yew that
ringed the house. Mottled
locust leaves floated on the air,
landed on his shirt, his cap, the
chainsaw cooling on the grass, as
the sun shone through the
transparency of the last leaves
holding on, until they too would
take their turn, and fall.

FAILURES

He felt the patterned shadows
of the leaves and limbs upon
the warm gray bark, bright
as the whole autumn day, the
once green leaves now filled
with yellow light, the blue sky
behind the further gray-green
trees, the three transecting
horizontal wires that echoed
those erased where now his
writing wrote, balanced line by
line, one below the other,
the way he sought to sift and
fill the chaos in his heart, the
failures stacked like bricks,
leaned one upon another, a
testament to knowing nothing
when correctness had come
due—his was a debt accrued
for what he could not do: be
the one that those who needed
love could lean upon, and
count steadfastness as his virtue,
to love without the judgment
loosed when they too found
they could not love; he felt the
failure he knew he would lift up
and bear again, and knew the
scale he weighed himself
upon would forever miss
the mark.

He felt the exhaustion, the dis-ease,
of the effort of protection, of trying
to block with one's body, one's
being, the momentum of the world,
the working of the celestial fire,
that sent out in every direction, the
manifestation of what is, unplanned,
arriving with no intent, with no
latent plan, but only pure being,
minted with the stamp of the new,
the never seen, all of it arriving
like the air, the light, the miraculous
formation of cells, invisible biological
births, in rhythms of intractable life;
and from this galactic, geological
thrust, the weight of the exponential
stardust, its imperative completeness,
to imagine, to conceive, to separate
out his own self, to stand against,
to shift aside, what arrived instant
after instant, that was in its coming
the only way he could continue
to be: his food, his sustenance, his
corporeal body built; to block or
refuse, to divert, to think he could
hold away, what arrived in its power,
its overwhelmingness, might be his
death—but was as certainly,
incomprehensibly, love.

JEWELS

The past, so-called, became
a chest filled with jewels,
precious and brilliant, into
which he dipped his hands
like a basin of jeweled water;
streams of sapphire and ruby,
emerald and gold ran through
his fingers: each gem one
encapsulated moment, a
particle of particular past,
which when held to the lamp
of the sky, flared out one
moment's infinity of pain or
pleasure, suffering or joy,
beauty or ugliness—an
entire world, that looked
backward and forward. But
here between finger and thumb
shone one micro-moment of
now, reflecting only itself,
which held in its presence the
jeweled caskets yet to be, being
built right then as he turned
around, as the eight directions
circled about, as zenith and nadir
climbed and receded, as his
small life fell away, revealing
true life: So his joy, his well
being became immense, as
he replaced the jewel with the
others, and slowly closed
the lid.

THE POWERLESS

I felt the powerlessness, the
inability of the good to prevail,
to be the victor in wars of
good against evil, the down-
trodden over greed, the wealthy
over the poor—as though wars
and victories over others were
not what we had to leave behind,
but to accept what we were,
that the poor were the poor,
and the wealthy the wealthy.
We wanted our own sort of
greed to triumph, we wanted *our*
power, *our* peacefulness, to
prevail; yet the only way was
release, the giving up, of what—
if we pushed and we shoved—
could only be grasped for
a moment, until, as it always
has, the scythe swept through,
and rich and poor were reaped
together. Yet there are times a
man, a woman, must stand up,
must shout before their fall:
"No more!"—though there *will*
be more, and more unending;
yet Truth is recognized, as
sunlight is, clear and bright, and
falsehood and its evil ways—
greed, unconcern, are also seen,
then fade into the nothingness,
the night.

BRIGHTNESS

The light was so bright,
so clear, it blinded; it could
be no brighter and still reveal,
the blindness was the looking
into, directly, and the brilliance,
the dazzling dance of light
was the looked-upon, where
the world leapt into being,
came forth in fullness,
in absolute presentness,
showering the world, the sight,
the eyes, the awareness,
the beauty, with astonishment
that *things could be*, that *these*
things could be: bark, leaves,
tree, sky; the chair at the table,
the computer on the desk,
the watch on his wrist. Outside,
past the clear window's glass,
one distillation, last night's
condensation, contracted to
a single drop, danced on the tip
of a hanging leaf, where the
light leapt, drawn to the sphere
and refracted out, ablaze—
now ruby, now gold, now
sapphire, even the sun itself,
complete in a pinpoint; and the
sky shone blue, and the eyes
that saw all of it were bright.

WINGS OF MORNING

Were all your difficulties not
my own, did not your afflictions
fall on me as well, and my own
upon you? Who among us escapes
our own individual pain, our
particular illness of the heart
and body, that seems ours alone
to bear in the vast wake of one's
long or short life—yet, what
is our red blood but the river,
the ocean of our mutual sea, that
bears us from our continent to
yours, in these frail boats of our
bodies, reaching across what
looks like emptiness, like space,
to touch fingers in the wings of
morning, light breaking past ragged
clouds over the frost, white on the
roofs of our warm huddled homes,
aching for dawn, for our selves
to drop the insularity of night,
and move again in the day's
bright air, where we become, by
our white billowed breath,
what we swore we were not,
the world.

THE UNCONCERNED

Thankfully the morning was
just the morning, sunlight
falling on the wind-shifting
leaves, moving the clouds
along in stately procession,
with no hint of opinion or
proclamation, no attitude or
lack of one. The light seemed
to arrive horizontally, though
he knew with his mind that
the sun was higher above
the horizon; still it intrigued
and fascinated him, that the
leaning limbs of the tree
could be lit from below,
rather than above, in the
same way that interior light
might come from any angle,
striking a new revelation,
another way of seeing what
one had seen many times
before—but now arrived in a
new way, creating in fact
a newness out of what was
thought of as old; but thank-
fully, the light, the morning,
did not care, as the light came
and went, brightening or
darkening the trees, as the
clouds moved on.

SINCERITY OF BEING

The leaves were thinner now,
papery, filled with brown-gold
light, dancing a bit in the breeze.
Thin dark branches, inked lines
against the pale blue-white of
the sky, these were the truth of
the tree, the root reality, *sky-roots*,
though their bareness implied
the cold, the winter to come;
they came forth with their
own honesty, their sincerity,
their unawareness of any way
to create pretense, their inability
to falsify, to not be who they
were, in the world, in themselves.
This is the world that was, that is,
that has always given what men
could not—absolute sincerity
of being; there was no work in it,
no need to strive, to combat a
weaker nature, to fear what gave
them life, to shrink from what
they lived within—and in this way
were silent teachers of men, of
myself, allowing that which
resonated within, that which *loved*,
to grow as they grew, and in my,
in our turn, give out as they did—
to the world, to the hearts of man.

The words, he felt, obscured, as
at the same time some revealed,
and it became a task of separation,
as of stones on the beach, the white
from the black, the large from the
small; yet this too exposed
artificiality, a point of view, an
ordering of the universe that denied
the given order, where all things
arrived together, and only an
analytical eye, a mind of obsession,
sought to make order, by grouping
what seemed the same, from what
seemed not to belong. And he saw
his unease with *the way things were*,
the need to shift reality to align
with his preference, his desire, so
that he wondered, why can I not
leave things alone? But the words
(for this was where he started) when
left to themselves did their own
sorting, the way the wind mixed
maple leaves with ash, willow with
walnut, and the patterns of November
dazzled the eye, in its own ordered
disorder, and its truth was apparent,
its unintentionality soothed the
heart and settled the soul. And he
said: words, whoever let you loose,
do what you will.

STRUCK

The leaves, turned for some
time, of the maple, the oak, lit by
the afternoon light, shattered the air,
the eye, in color alight like no
other, only their own with the sky
behind, crystalline and pale blue, the
air stripped of otherness, only the
instantaneous transmission of
luminous ether, from interstellar
to earthly receptor; one was
struck dumb, dropped to the knees
felt by Saints upon stones,
hands folded, eyes lifted upward
as angels descend, yet the only
action was to be struck stone still,
movement arrested, unbelievableness
standing present in the everyday,
there, with the everything else—
cars moving down the street,
people walking this way and that,
geese heading west before they
turned south; so the procession
proceeded, the unnoticed noted by
few, you could hardly say it
mattered, another fall day—yet it
fell, it landed, as unlikely as
any fiery chariot out of the sky, the
ordinary unveiled; bliss beheld in
one simple moment's blessing.

SOLARIS

The light was running horizontally,
falling right to left, long lines
of alternating stripes, dark
and light, running behind barns,
shooting over the rise of a hill,
pulling corn stubble straight up and
then laying it down by the thousand-
fold; it blinded your eyes; you had to
look up, or down, in order just to see,
which wasn't a bad thing, to see
right where you stood, feet below you
holding you up, your head already
partway into the sky, while straight
ahead hung Solaris, the great illuminator,
burning out your eyeballs, so you
close them tight, and green amorphous
clouds glow in a black reforming
field, but if you turn away, your
back to the brightness, what rushes
up is so clear, created in that instant,
by a brush dipped in clarity, painted
liquid morning air, all crystalness, all
demarcation and sharpness, as your
hands sink inside your pockets, as your
breath billows out, softening the
white edges of the air.

UNCHANGING

He had no certainty in
the way things were, only
in the way things were in
this particular moment, for
they changed, they transformed
in the next into something
that seemed, from the outside,
unsimilar, so that he could
never say, with certainty, *this*
is the way things are, always.
The best he could do was
agree with the Buddhists, that
everything changes, that nothing
stays the same. Then he saw
it, what he wrote, and almost
laughed at the truth of it:
nothing stays the same. *Some
thing* always changes. You
almost could miss it again,
even when you knew what to
look for, and so the anxiety
he was feeling relaxed; it was
like running into an old friend,
someone you loved, who loved
you, on the cold streets of a
strange city; you embraced
and sat on a park bench,
feeling the mutual comfort,
warming you both, as your
worries slipped away.

Not yet, the not knowing
says, now is not the time
to know, this is what I've
given—uncertainty—as your
mind tries to scale the glass
mountain, impenetrable;
not glass, but quartz, not
quartz but diamond, clear,
all the way through, but no
way to get in or out, not by
looking for a door, for a key;
frozen in the this or that,
wanting a way—your way—
when ways, plans, paths,
maps and agendas, are
destinations past, continents
left behind, earlier stages of
evolution, your childhood,
your schoolyards, your old
ways of loving: what is coming
you can't know, it has no
existence, the formless has
nothing to offer, as something
arrayed in the future, only
this arriving now, gone as
you try to grab on, arriving
again and again, unknown,
brilliant and new.

He was crossing an unknown
land, one he no longer knew,
though the landmarks were
identifiable and familiar; it was
the mystery of what stretched
before him, as the distance
lessened, as time in the outward
sense contracted, but inwardly
expanded and deepened, as
goals and achievements hour
by hour, day by day, lost their
imperative, and what he had once
set as a destination had been
passed with only slight remarking.
Now he had no *where* to go, and
the distance between somewhere
and nowhere was steadily
decreasing; in a similar manner
his excitement, his sense of
the immensity of some thing he
could not name grew, as though
that which he searched for
his whole life unknowing, and
which he called by many names,
which had been refracted by
art, music, certain writings; by
beautiful women, by men of
gravity and honor, drew near, but
was none of these. And he felt the
thrill, and it hummed in the air.

SACRIFICE

The direction seemed to lead
either toward the fear, external
and increasing, and by involvement
with the outer only add to what
grew larger on its own—or follow
the path inward and down, in
what looked like retreat and
withdrawal, but by all he had so
far come to trust, knew was the
territory of the real, of the true,
though it offered no apparent
reprieve, or solution to the chaos
that was forming outward and
above. The old voices spoke
behind him, of responsibility, of
valor, of sacrifice—and they had
a partial truthfulness that pulled;
yet all they asked were bodies for
their funeral pyres, and in this he
felt no honor, only the obligation of
the herd, to offer himself up in
sacrifice; and so he chose inward
and downward, through veils and
darknesses, without any clear
reason why other than allegiance
to a scent, a sense, of something he
once called soul, or spirit, or the
guidance of an angel, but now he
followed only for its light.

He realized that he was simply
one point of view, one perspective,
one reflection of everything that
was, like a crystal that flashed
forth the light it gathered,
it filled and informed him, its
particular angles and refractions,
the unique form of his growth,
his shape, his sensitivities—all
these meant nothing the way he had
thought they did, they were the
container that offered the world
a way in to who he was, and then,
like the crystal, a way out.
These flashes, these reflections
and emanations, were the Light;
he was only the light that filled his
being, and his being was the light
offered back, warmed by some aspect
of his own uniqueness, but his, only
one leaf in a forest, offering his
brightness from his green beginning
to his orange and gold blaze. And
now the winter was come, the
first snow, as the wind's roar
whispered peace, as the rest and
renewal of silence, as the crystals
of snow began to fall.

WHAT EMERGED

Would there be a place
he could stop, he wondered;
there had never been a plan,
a beginning, a middle, an end;
all of it was what it was,
what emerged, the way the
darkness outside the window
had emerged from the gray
pre-winter light of the
November day. Even now
he could feel it falter, this
stream that fed the flow that
ran out into the room, climbing
his legs, his chest and arms,
seeking the page and moving
on, a dissatisfied animal
searching and not finding the
scent, what it needed for
nourishment. It wandered away
and he watched it go, leaving
only the disorganized trail
in the dry leaves, This is what
it was like: nothing beyond
the ordinary, moving up, over
and around him, as he tried
to write some of it down,
as it turned and looked into his
face, eyes glinting without
recognition, wild and unknowing.
All he could do was look back.

BREATHING UNDER WATER

He sat in the morning silence,
and the more attention he gave
to it, the more it enveloped,
filling the room and the walls,
the window and his chair, the
way that slow water rises, or fog
envelops a valley, only here the
silence did not obscure but
brought clarity and distinctness.
Only the small noises, water in
the pipes, the ticking of the
clock intruded; his breakfast
moving in his stomach, small
ticks that came from the furniture,
the beams of the old house. It
was as though he moved into
it at the same moment it moved
into him, erasing the edges of
all he described, loosening any
sense of himself as separate,
of himself as *he*. Now it was as
though breathing under the water,
totally immersed and saturated,
and all he knew was the freedom
he felt, like wings on the open
air, total interpenetration, and the
gift of moving anywhere with
complete ease, at the same time
he moved nowhere at all, as
he sat silent, in the silence.

MEMORY

All of it was odd, what he
remembered of his life, the
memories that seemed so real;
that there was a time, or the many
moments, when the remembered
was occurring, when he lived
in different bodies—smaller,
more energetic, then larger
and insecure, afraid of so much
in the world. He could not feel
in this moment if those moments
had been real; some of them
were lit by presence, most were
like a dream, like swimming
under water. The room, as he
looked about him, held that same
quality: real at the moment of
attention, unreal as a dream
when he looked away. Outside
the window, yesterday's snow
had disappeared; the brilliant
colors of the leaves were nowhere
to be seen. He felt the solid floor
beneath him, but everything had
a sense of softening, of fading
imperceptibly away. Yet the
paper felt real, and the pencil—
but the words, where were
the words coming from? Where
were they going?

THE POSSIBILITY

The morning was giving him
nothing, but he felt optimism
in the empty space that gathered
around the trees and stones, the
sounds of machinery, automobiles
driving by, airplanes flying
overhead. The free movement
of the birds was part of it, the
undirectedness of the clouds,
forming and unforming in the
sky; all of this opened possibility
to him, the unrestrictedness that
allowed him, his soul, to move
wherever it wished, traveling on
the beams of light that fell as
the creation of the needles of the
pine, the bark of the maple. It
was not so much what he *would*
accomplish as that he *could*
accomplish; and that was the
gift, made manifest by awareness,
by being aware, of its possibility,
and in the things that *were*, of
their utter impossibility, their
miraculousness, their arresting
beauty, that flowed forth without
effort as the breath of the world's
being, of which he was a particle,
participant, evanescence, alive in
the tumbling creativity of the
moment, even as he sat unmoving,
loving it all.

LIGHT INTO BREATH

The quality of the light had
its effect: the clarity in the
pale blue of the sky, not
the direct rays that you would
notice, but a kind of sparkle,
an activation of the air itself,
as though shot through with
aliveness, an excitation of
energy in the molecules
themselves, a dance of the
everywhere element of *prana*,
the breath, extended from the
sun-source to the earth-inhaling
beings: men, plants, animals,
insects. All this was carried
on light, extending its tendrils
into every crevice, even to
its transformation at the
boundaries of non-light, the
darkness where the energies
turned inward, a phosphorescent
illumination, black-light of the
soul of creation, womb waiting
for the birthing to leap outward
to the light—both floated in
finger-touch, right at that edge,
energized and passing their
vibratory aliveness from
the velvet nothingness to the
intensification of discriminated
being—light into dark, night
into day.

THE AIR OF HISTORY

He felt the memories melt
away from him, and before
leaving he sensed how strong
his attachment was, how each
one had been polished like a
jewel, and his desire to hold
it fast, to keep it locked away
where only he could possess
it, was strong, almost over-
powering. But they were going,
and somehow that had to
happen, if he were to step
away from what held him
prisoner, frozen in the robotic
wax image of himself; yet the
memories—those were who he
was, they built him out the
air of history, the trajectory
of image; and who was he now,
without the fantasy of *what
was*? The room presented itself
in the evening lamp-light, the
curtains closed to the wind and
arriving snow; here *he* sat,
undiscoverable, as was the
chair, the bed, the bookcase.
Everything that called to him
was a memory in retreat,
a recollection, an echo that
dimmed and faded as he
listened, as the hot water ticked
in the pipes, and the sounds of
cars passed by unseen
on the road.

WHAT HE LOVED

What can be held onto,
he wondered, and he knew
the answer, the one he didn't
like—that there was nothing.
Nothing could be grasped
against going; all would
go, as so much had already
gone: age, beauty, wealth—
the dreams of security, his
children doing well in the
world; of the Buddha's
litany of birth, aging, sickness
and death: it was all so much
sand sifting through his
fingers, even as it seemed to
persist, to parade past, a
display of the unattainable,
the illusory, a taunt and a
tease, drawing him out and
away from acceptance and
allowing that *all these were
so*; and he greatly desired to
let go, to sink in, to dissolve,
to cease from his endless
efforts to form a solid shell
around, to become in the end
what he loved: the wind, the
open air, the sunlight spread
across the fields, the space
that traveled on and on
and held so easily, the stars.

HIS OWN WAY

In the morning light he
saw how he favored his own
way, not in the sense of
placing himself first,
in greater importance or
knowledge, but in the
manner of wandering alone,
he and his own thoughts,
the intimacy with what some
called the greater mind,
the world, that he could
only find in the absence of
others, away from their
distractions, their multiple
varied outward directions;
and he recalled the way
the world spoke to him,
wordlessly, in the presence
of the overlooked, the crystal
sheltered in the rock, the
curled leaf abandoned by
the tree, the first buds before
they broke open in spring,
the caws of the crows
as they flew, their black triads,
from tree to tree. And he felt
the strength flow back into
his being, though it had never
left, and he looked up at
the radiance in the sheeted
clouds, thick with gratitude,
with wonder.

ANTIDOTE

The gold glowed on the
wall next to the window,
outshone by the brightness
of last night's snow-filled
whiteness. K told him he
needed yellow, and he had
none; so with palette knives
and paint he drew that
radiance from the inside
out. Unframed, it was no
masterpiece, but the alchemy
of color worked its own
magic upon him—reaching
out from the shadow of
the wall; it entered his heart,
not the eyes, and he felt
as though veils, wrapping his
chest like tissue, were
burning away—until looking
at the painting was like
looking at his own body: a
vast field of dandelion
blossoms waving in rhythms
of cadmium; and where
the white winter was peace,
and a sleep of the external, the
yellow blazed with the
radiance of the sun, and from
within him spread aliveness
and joy, as he joined the
real rushing outward to
be born.

FASCINATION

He wondered if it were
all about wonder, the
wandering here and there,
the way he did as a child,
in fascination with the
things he found, usually
small, insignificant, at
least from an adult's point
of view—sticks and odd
stones, bugs, the ridges
on the underside of a leaf,
old paint, cracked and
curled on the wood siding
of a garage, bits of glass
gleaming in the gravel,
weeds of all kinds, unnamed
seeds, prickly and profligate,
the pit of a half-eaten peach, the
hornets that buzzed around,
the damp world of slugs
under a flat stone, the
reticulated moss that grew
under dripping water, how
a dragonfly hovers, or the
appearances of images
on window glass, a dry
version of frost, lit by the
summer sun—all these and the
undiscovered more, drew
him step by step, deeper
into the world that needed no
reason, other than to be there,

mysterious and beckoning,
calling him to look, and
since he was there,
he saw.

He looked at the blank
page, and knew by the
time it was filled, already
at this point begun, that
he would have gone from
anxiousness to peace, from
a place of unsettledness to
calm. A quarter of the way
there he paused, feeling
the fear flood back in,
like a napkin soaking up
water spilled on a table.
At the halfway point—
see, *we've arrived there*
together—it was like
watching a glass being
slowly filled with water;
he marveled, that, where
only moments ago there
was nothing, now the glass
was almost three-quarters
full. Here again he paused,
bent over, leaning on his
knees, taking a breath.
As the pencil pushed off,
he knew he was almost
there, but what would the
difference be? Was the page
filled any different than the
page empty? Then the wind
rose, curling the letters,
and he watched them all
blowing away.

ALLOWING

The light from the lamp
was too harsh, too bright,
yet without it, the light
from the windows was
harder to see by, to place
the written words, but it
was more reassuring, more
loving in its soft way, so
that the words came with
gentleness, and gathered
with a soft grayness on the
page. Outside the window
the snow was melting, the
sky was a pale slate, and
he sat with the intention
to let his mind disengage,
to allow, by not resisting
the flow of the day over
and about him; to allow
himself to join in, to relax
in the slow seep of that
movement, as the branches
in the trees moved only
if you looked long enough,
as the hands on the clock
did their minute revolving
dance, as the shadows in
the room shortened. His
foot at the end of his leg,
crossed over the other knee,
bobbed in a tiny rhythm
to the beat of his heart.

He leaned forward into a day
that brought its own
invitations, and that listened
to none of his own.

LOSS

More and more he felt
that those things he thought
he controlled, those powers
he believed he once had, were
slipping away; his capacities
to do diminished, his thoughts
multiplied and went in their
own directions, his ability
to remain one-pointed, to
meditate, ended in sleep. He
judged himself harshly, but
letting that go, he found he
ended up with less and less,
whereas when he was younger
his imagination told him, by
this time, he would be stronger,
more focused, accomplished
in wisdom and knowledge.
Yet here he was, a snowman
melting away, a cadaver
eaten by crows, until only the
bones were left, and those
gnawed by wolves and dogs.
This black mood matched
the time of year, and that was
reassuring: to understand
that everything is stripped
away before anything new
can be born.

THE WATCHER

The deep snow, melted
away to bare earth, returns
barely a week into winter,
as a dust of white, a hard-
frozen frost, under a gray
sky that asks nothing but
to be as you are, letting
it all in as you have, as
you are doing now. Sit, it
says, like the hawk on the
high wire, watching as
the wind raises its feathers,
as the field runs away in
plowed stubbled rows, as the
light climbs over the thin
furrows of snow. Somewhere,
a mouse has not yet moved,
still feels its pea-sized heart
beat within its warm
brown body, watches, past
the mown stalks of wheat,
the white wind gather
the world's day, blowing it
down the field and over
the hills toward town.

THE WORDS

He wanted to give all the
words up, or to wring them
out, like wet laundry, of
all their old meanings, of
the way the words dictated
the meaning—he wanted
the meaning to come first,
to let the words be the
scaffold, the way he could
bridge the distance between
what he felt, and himself
again—someone, who could
be you, reading the words
on the page. The words were
like air that carried the seed,
the life of the plant, its
incipient being, from one
place to another, to the soil
where it would rest, would
germinate, would grow into
a full life, green and vibrant.
The words were the way
across an emptiness; yet
he sensed this was only a
partial truth, for the emptiness
connected everything—*being*
everything—so that in
another way no words were
needed at all. Perhaps,
only in the beginning,
until we learned, at last, to
speak without them.

THE ARRIVAL

Before dawn, billowing
gray clouds and a cold wind
over thin snow. Something
rises up, as it always has, to
greet what comes, a new being,
never met before, who comes
only to you; a powerful being,
filled with secrets, with
knowledge of other lands,
of vast distances, of worlds
hard to believe. He arrives on,
he brings with him, the light,
and his mystery is felt in the
darkness before he arrives,
before the light can betray his
newness; he puts on his
ordinary clothes, old, worn,
rough clothes of the world—so
he arrives unseen, one of the
thousands who has passed before.
But beneath the wrinkles and
the dirt, the old hat and the
firm set smile, *he is* the wonder,
the excitement in your heart.
You search for him at the
station, among all the others,
fearful he has passed, that
perhaps you have missed him.
Yet when the crowd thins he
stands where he arrived, waiting
by himself, waiting for you.

ABOUT THE AUTHOR

Richard Wehrman has been a painter, jewelry design-
er, graphic designer, award-winning illustrator, and
writer. He has been a student of Zen Buddhism, the
School of Spiritual Psychology, and the Diamond Ap-
proach. He lives with his wife in Upstate New York.
This is his fourth book of poetry.

✳

This collection gathers poems written in 2016. They
were a written exploration utilizing the practice of
Inquiry as practiced in the Diamond Approach, and
strongly influenced by the style of the remarkable
book, "The Death of Virgil", written in 1945 by the
Austrian author Hermann Broch.

✳

48978232R00058

Made in the USA
Middletown, DE
03 October 2017